Enrichment Series
Advanced Bible Study
No. E-2

Teach Us To Pray

A study of the Scriptural Principles of Prayer

**by
Elaine Dull and Jo Anne Sekowsky**

AGLOW BIBLE STUDIES

Aglow Bible Studies

Creation (#1)
A Study of Genesis 1-11

God's Daughter (#2)
Practical Aspects of a Christian Woman's Life

Fruit of the Spirit (#3)
A Guide to the Production and Maturing of Godly Fruit

The Gifts of the Spirit (#4)
A Study of Spiritual Gifts in the Body of Christ

Basic Beliefs (#5)
A Primer of Christian Doctrine

Patterns for Parents (#6)
A Study in Parent-Child Relations as Seen in Scripture

God's Answer to Overeating (#7)
A Study of Scriptural Attitudes

Ministries for Women (#8)
Old and New Testament Examples of Women in Ministry

The Call of Jesus (#9)
Lessons in Becoming His Disciple

Christ in You (#10)
A Study of the Book of Colossians

A Place for God to Live (#11)
A Blueprint for Christian Living Pictured in the Tabernacle

Triumph Through Temptation (#12)
How to Conquer Satan's Lies

Wholeness From God (#E-1)
Patterns and Promises for Health and Healing

ATTENTION

These studies have been published for the edification of every Christian and may be used by any individual or group. However, unless a Bible study group is in contact with a local Women's Aglow Fellowship and is under its leadership, the name "Aglow" cannot be used in any way to designate the study group.

© Copyright 1979, Women's Aglow Fellowship, Lynnwood, Washington USA All rights to this book are reserved. No part of this book may be reproduced in any manner whatsoever without written permission of Women's Aglow Fellowship.
Printed in the United States of America
ISBN 0-930756-49-5

Table of Contents

1. Does God Hear our Prayers? 5
2. Love 10
3. How to Pray 16
4. What Can We Pray For? 24
5. Praying in the Spirit 31
6. Praise and Thanksgiving 37
7. Intercessory Prayer 44
8. Fasting 51
9. Esther 57

All references in this study are taken from the New American Standard Bible unless noted as follows: KJV (King James Version), TLB (The Living Bible), TAB (The Amplified Bible).

Introduction

"Lord, teach us to pray." How many of us have echoed this request made by Jesus' disciples? Few aspects of the Christian life have so continuously perplexed generation after generation of Christians, and too many Christians today honestly admit that their prayer life is less than satisfactory.

Our very questions on the subject betray our confusion.

How important is prayer?

How can we know whether we are praying according to God's will?

Why are some prayers answered and others not?

Can we actually hinder our own prayers?

Where does faith come in?

Does praying more than once about a request show a lack of faith?

Does continual prayer about a want or need amount to vain repetition?

How important is our attitude when we pray?

Do we come boldly before the throne of God or do we approach our Creator humbly?

What does it mean to pray in the Spirit?

Do we bring all concerns to God, or shouldn't we bother Him with our trivial everyday problems?

How does fasting relate to prayer?

When are we supposed to pray for others?

A casual reading of the Bible can give the impression of confusing, even contradictory information about prayer. However, we can rest assured that a loving Father would not shroud in mystery a subject as important as prayer.

Learning to pray is a matter of study and practice, effort and time. The Bible teaches definite principles of prayer, and a comprehensive study will not only answer our questions about prayer but will yield us the precious fruit of a glorious time spent in the presence of God, where His will and ours are one, and our prayers are answered.

This Bible study has been written to be used by women in groups or those studying individually. It is written for all Christian women who are not completely satisfied with their prayer life, women who in their hunger for the things of the Lord want to touch the very heart of God with their prayers.

Lesson One

Does God Hear Our Prayers?

Introduction
Before we can even begin to pray, we must silence our doubts and find the answers to some perplexing questions. First, exactly what is prayer? Defined in its simplest terms, prayer is communication with God. This brings up another question: what then is communication?

Communication is always a two-way process, an interchange. You speak and then listen to the other person's response. He speaks and in turn listens. Communication with God is no different. We are communicating with a Person who both listens (and if we will listen, replies). Oh, but that explanation hits at the very heart of one of our gravest doubts. Although we have spoken to God on many occasions, how can we know that He hears those prayers?

Prayer: Lord, as we begin this study on prayer, we can only echo the words of the disciples, "Teach us to pray." Amen

Discussion Question: Does God hear all prayers, those of both Christians and non-Christians alike?

Bible Study
Read **Psalms 3:4, 4:3, 6:8-9, 10:17, 17:6, 34:4, 38:15, 40:1, 120:1** and **John 11:41-42.**

(1)   All of these Scriptures tell us that God does _____.

The people praying in the above verses were in different states and different conditions, which might represent some of the times and ways we call upon God.

(2)   How did the psalmist pray in Psalm 3:4? _____.

(3)   What was his condition in Psalm 6:8-9? _____

       In Psalm 34:4? _____.

(4)   What was his condition in Psalm 40:1? _____.

       In Psalm 120:1? _____.

In Psalm 40:1? _____.

In Psalm 120:1? _____.
(5) In Psalm 4:3 and Psalm 17:6, the psalmist has faith that the

Lord will hear him whenever he _____.
(6) What is the result of the Psalmist's knowing the Lord will

answer his prayer in Psalm 38:15? He _____ in the Lord.

Discussion Question: When are the times you are most likely to call upon the Lord?

Read **John 11: 41-44.**
(7) What miracle was Jesus expecting His Father to perform when

He prayed? _____.

(8) Why does Jesus say he is praying? _____
_____
_____.

(9) When does He say God hears him? _____.

(10) Was Jesus' prayer answered? _____.

    Certainly, the above Scriptures give us ample evidence that the Lord does indeed hear our prayers when we pray.

    In the face of such overwhelming evidence, we must reject any doubts we may have that God hears our prayers. However, before we can proceed further, we need to clear up one more concern. Although God is willing to hear our prayers, does He really want them or does He just hear them because He is so loving? In other words, how do our prayers appear to God?

Read **Revelation 5:8** and **Revelation 8:3-4.**
(11) How does the writer describe our prayers? _____
_____.

Read **Proverbs 15:8.**
(12) How is our prayer described in this verse? _____.
    Although incense is not necessarily in vogue in our modern society, its fragrance is pleasing to the Lord. We can be assured that our prayers ascend to God as a "sweet smelling savor" and are a delight to Him.

Read **Psalm 139.**

(13) In this Psalm, the writer leads us one step further. How often is God thinking about us? _____.

(14) When are some of the times God is thinking about us?

_____

_____

_____.

Let's summarize what we've learned so far. We worship a God who always _____ our prayers and is constantly _____ about us. To him, our prayers are as _____.

Discussion Question: What do you consider your biggest problem regarding prayer and how are you handling it at this time?

Now that we've come this far let's take a look at some of the smaller questions which perplex many of us. Is there a special time of day when God wants us to pray? a preferred position of prayer? a place? Do we pray to the Father or to Jesus?

These may seem laughable questions to some, but to others who want to know everything the Bible has to say on prayer, they are very real concerns.

Let's look at the question of to whom we pray first. Does it matter?

Read **John 16:23**.

(15) To whom does Jesus say to pray? _____. In whose name are we to pray? _____.

Read **Luke 11:1-2**.

(16) To whom is this prayer addressed? _____
Jesus clearly indicates that we are to pray to the Father in His Name. However, no one should come under bondage in this matter. We worship one God in three persons. If, for example, you are comfortable only praying to Jesus, make this concern a matter of prayer. Ask the Lord what you should do.

Our next questions concern the when and where of prayer.

Read **Psalm 55:17** and **Psalm 5:3**.

(17) When does the Psalmist say he prays? _____.

Read **Psalm 32:6**.

(18) When does he indicate he had prayed in this verse? _____

_____.

Read **Psalm 42:8**.

(19) What time is indicated here? _____.

Read **Psalm 86:7.**
(20) What does this verse have to say? _____.

Read **Ephesians 6:18.**
(21) When does the Apostle Paul urge us to pray? _____.

Read **Luke 18:1.**
(22) Why does the writer say Jesus told this story? _____.

Read **1 Thessalonians 5:17.**
(23) How often are we told to pray? _____.

Discussion Question: How do you think we pray "without ceasing"?

Read **1 Timothy 2:8.**
(24) Where does the Apostle tell us to pray in this verse? _____.

Is there one position of prayer that is more acceptable to God than others?

Read **1 Timothy 2:8, Acts 7:60** and **Matthew 26:39.**
(25) What positions of prayer are mentioned in these three verses?

_____.

We have covered a lot of ground in this chapter, but it has all been necessary. Our study has shown us what a truly wonderful God we have. Not only does he hear and delight in our prayers, but he finds them acceptable at all times, in all places.

Personal Application

(1) What misconceptions about God's attitude toward my prayers has hindered my prayer life?
(2) If I have trouble hearing God's voice, is it because I don't stop and listen for it?
(3) If God is thinking about me all the time, what is my responsibility to him?

Notebook Assignment

Start a prayer diary which you will keep throughout this entire study. A regular spiral or loose-leaf notebook will do. Buy one just for the occasion; don't fall into the trap of using scraps of paper — they always get lost.

Use the first one-half of your notebook for diary-type writing. The second half will be for different prayer experiments, of keeping track of your prayers and the date they are answered.

For a beginning, try to include the four types of prayer—praise and worship, petition, thanksgiving and meditation, in your prayer time each day. Every time you specifically pray for someone or something, write it down, the date you first prayed about this concern and finally the date on which your prayer is answered.

You might also want to try a new experiment in prayer, such as getting up half an hour before your family and using that time for prayer. Or perhaps you have never prayed on your face. One person shared how the Bible really became more alive to her when she read it on her knees in a prayerful attitude, always keeping a pencil and paper handy to write down anything the Lord revealed to her during this time.

Another good idea is to either pick a prayer partner from your Bible study group and agree to specifically pray for one another's needs for the duration of the Bible study, or to pray for each member of the study group every day. Find out what the needs of the other group members are and specifically pray about these things, of course remembering to jot down the requests, the date, and the date the prayer is answered.

Advanced Studies

(1) Make a thorough study of the book of Psalms, looking for examples of the many times the psalmist sought the Lord in prayer.
(2) Divide your material into the four categories of prayer: praise and worship, petition, thanksgiving, and meditation. Which type(s) of prayer predominate?
(3) Analyze your own prayer life. Is it unbalanced? If so, consciously try to strike a better balance among the different types of prayer.

Enrichment Assignment for Chapter 2.

(1) Study the following Scriptures: **Exodus 22:18; Leviticus 19:26, 31, 20:27; Deuteronomy 18:9-14; Acts 16:16-18; Revelation 21:8** to learn God's attitude toward all forms of the occult.
(2) Read **Psalm 133:1; Proverbs 12:20, 17:17, 25:21-22; Matthew 5:5, 7, 9; Luke 6:35-38; John 13:35; Romans 12:9-21; 1 Corinthians 13; 2 Corinthians 5:17, 13:11; 1 Peter 3:8-11; 1 John 1:7, 2:10, 3:14, 4:12;** What does God say about loving others?

Memory Work

(If you prefer another version of the Bible, take your memory work from it.)

(1) "But know that the Lord has set apart the godly men for Himself; the Lord hears when I call to Him" (Ps. 4:3).
(2) "Pray without ceasing" (1 Thess. 5:17).
(3) "I waited patiently for the Lord; and He inclined to me, and heard my cry. He brought me up out of the pit of destruction, out of the miry clay; and He set my feet upon a rock, making my footsteps firm. And He put a new song in my mouth, a song of praise to our God; many will see and fear, and will trust in the Lord" (Ps. 40:1-3).

Lesson Two

Love

Introduction

The fact that Jesus has commanded us to love Him and one another shows His intimate knowledge of His creatures. Everyone is in favor of love, yet few of us know how to love and if God did not ask it of us, few would be willing to pay the great price that love requires. Somehow, there is a gap between what our heart knows to be right and what our emotions lead us to do.

Just what does love have to do with getting our prayers answered? Perhaps it is not too surprising that Jesus tied the two together. In fact, the very success of our prayer life depends in a large part on how well we obey his command.

Prayer: Lord, open the ears of our heart today, so we may truly hear what You are teaching us. Amen.

Discussion Question: How has using my prayer notebook changed my praying?

Bible Study

Read **1 John 3:22-23**.
(1) How do we receive what we pray for? _____

_____

_____

(2) What is God's commandment? _____

_____

Read **Matthew 22:37-40**.
Jesus took all the instruction of the Old Testament and all His own teachings and put them into two commandments.
(3) What are the two great commandments? _____

_____

Discussion Question: What do you think "loving your neighbor as yourself" means?

The world usually has its priorities upside down. There are many people who feel how we treat "our neighbors" is much more important than worshiping God. However, God demands top priority in our lives. Even though some people in the world display a kind of love that puts many Christians to shame, nevertheless, they still miss the boat because they do not love God first.

Discussion Question: Why do you think God insists that we put Him first?

The first four commandments that God gave to Moses concern our relationship to Him.
Read **Exodus 20:1-11.**
(4) What are these first four commandments? _____

_____

_____

_____.

Discussion Question: What are some areas in your life where you do not put God first?

The Old Testament is all too frequently the story of the Israelites' trying to live without God and worshiping idols. An idol can be any object of ardent or excessive devotion or admiration. It can be a husband, child, job, hobby, possession, ambition. Love of anything that detracts from our devotion to God is an idol.
(5) Do you have any idols in your life? If so, name them. _____

_____.

If our answer to the above question was "yes," we need to ask God's forgiveness and ask Him how we can put Him first in our "love life."

The other six commandments are concerned with our relationships with other people.
(6) What are the other commandments? _____

_____

_____

_____.

Ever since Adam and Eve ate the forbidden fruit, man has been trying to set up his own standards of right and wrong. But God has made

it plain what he thinks of these man-made standards.
Read 1 Corinthians 3:18-20.
(7) What does God consider the wisdom of the world? _____
(8) Can you think of any way in which you are deviating from

God's standard of morality? _____

_____.

If the Holy Spirit has revealed any such area(s) in your life, ask the Lord's forgiveness right now and purpose in your heart to obey His standards.

When we begin to make up our own rules of right and wrong, we are actually idolizing our own intelligence! This is arrogance.

Discussion Question: Are common sense and God's wisdom the same thing? Why or why not?

Read Micah 6:8.
(9) What should our attitude as Christians be? _____

_____.

Read Philippians 2:1-5.
Many people have few problems in their Christian walk as long as they're alone. But, add just one person to the scene and sooner or later there will be conflict. However, **people** is what the Church is all about.

(10) What should our relationship to other Christians be? _____

_____.

Read Ephesians 4:21-32.
(11) Summarize the things mentioned here that were not mentioned

in the Philippians' passage. _____

_____

_____

_____

_____

_____.

These verses were not written to discourage us, but rather to show us what our goals should be.

One difficult area in the subject of relationships is unforgiveness.
Read Matthew 18:15.
(12) Who does this verse concern itself with? _____

(13) What are we supposed to do? _____

Read **Matthew 5:23-24.**
(14) Who does this verse concern itself with? _____

(15) What are we required to do? _____

Read **Mark 11:24-26.**
(16) What do these verses indicate may hinder the answer to our prayers? _____

(17) Does it matter who's at fault? _____
The natural man rebels at this. It's unfair! We feel we should only have to go halfway because there is usually fault on both sides. However, God doesn't take this into consideration. We are supposed to seek reconciliation regardless of who is at fault.

Discussion Question: Why do you think God put such a high priority on forgiveness?

Read **1 John 4:20-21.**
(18) What does this verse say we cannot do? _____

Read **1 John 3:16.**
(19) What is the proof of God's love for us? _____

(20) What should we be willing to do in return? _____

Read **1 John 3:17.**
(21) What is another test of our love (or lack of it)? _____

Discussion Question: What forms should our compassion take?

The apostle is saying that love is an action, rather than just a feeling. "Sloppy Agape" meets none of God's requirements for love.
Read **James 1:22.**

(22) What does James say we must be? _____
_____.

(23) If we are hearers of the Word only, what do we do to ourselves?
_____.

Genuine love finds its expression in practical ways. When we are carrying out this love, then our heart or our conscience should not condemn us. Sometimes, however, the devil, the slanderer, will try to make us feel guilty when we have no cause for guilt. We do not need to accept unwarranted feelings of guilt.

Discussion Question: Do I still carry around feelings of guilt over areas of my life or actions that God has forgiven years ago?

Read **1 John 3:20**.
(24) Who is still greater than our heart? _____.
Claiming this truth, we can come, in Jesus, with confidence before God and have anything we ask.
Read **James 5:16**.
(25) Who are we told to confess our sins to in this verse? _____
_____.

Sometimes, in addition to going directly to God for forgiveness, we must also confess our sins to one another and be prayed for by them.

Discussion Question: When do you think confession to a friend or group might be helpful?

God, in his great wisdom, has not only made love for Him and our fellow man His top priority, He has placed this love at the very center of answered prayer.

Personal Application
(1) Jesus said that the true test of love is our willingness to give up our life for someone. How does my love stack up against that standard?
(2) The Bible equates hatred with murder. Have I allowed hatred for anyone to erode my spiritual life?
(3) Is God truly first in my life?

Notebook Assignment
With God's help, make a list of anyone you have not truly forgiven. Make a second list of anyone who has reason to be offended with you. See if God would have you go see them (best), telephone (second best) or write (third best) those people, asking their forgiveness. **If you are willing,** be ready to share your experiences with your group the next time you meet.

List any forgiven areas of your life you still feel guilty over. Begin thanking God each day for forgiving you, that in His eyes your sin is as far away as the East is from the West. Continue to do this until you are completely aware of God's forgiveness. Record your feelings in your notebook.

Advanced Studies
(1) The Bible speaks mostly about three kinds of love: agape, philo and eros. Make a study of these three words and learn their essential differences.
(2) Much of God's wisdom is expressed in very practical form in Proverbs. Study one chapter of this book, comparing God's wisdom with the world's.
(3) Study 1 Samuel 15:22-23. What does God call rebellion and stubbornness? Relate these verses to what God has said about witchcraft and idolatry.

Enrichment Assignment for Chapter 3
(1) Take one of the Gospels and study it carefully concerning the occasions when Jesus prayed. See if you can learn any principles of prayer from this study.

Memory Work
(1) "If we confess our sins, He is faithful and righteous to forgive us our sins and to cleanse us from all unrighteousness" (1 John 1:9).
(2) ". . .Let us not love with word, or with tongue; but in deed and truth" (1 John 3:18).
(3) "Love is patient, love is kind, and is not jealous; love does not brag and is not arrogant, does not act unbecomingly; it does not seek its own, is not provoked, does not take into account a wrong suffered" (1 Cor. 13:4-5).

Lesson Three
How to Pray

Introduction
If we could only pray like Jesus! Our Lord was the most successful pray-er who ever lived. During His ministry here He tried to teach His followers (not only those who lived during His earthly lifetime, but the many who would come later) the secrets of answered prayer. Consequently, the Bible has some very definite instructions about prayer; it also gives many reasons why we do not always receive what we pray for. First we will look at the reasons for so-called unanswered prayer.

Prayer: Lord, we come to You today in the name of Jesus, confessing our ignorance about the kind of prayers that are pleasing to You. Give us understanding that we might learn Your secrets of prayer. Amen.

Discussion Question: Our notebook assignment was very personal. Is anyone willing to share how God worked in her life through this assignment?

Bible Study
Read **Psalm 66:18**
(1) What is one reason our prayers may not be answered? _____
_____.

Read **Jeremiah 7:1-16.**
(2) In v. 16, what does the Lord tell the prophet not to do? _____
_____.

(3) Verses 1-9 relate Judah's sins. Many of them are applicable to all

times and all places. What are some of these sins? _____

_____

_____

_____.

Dealing with unforgiven sin in our life is a recurring problem for all **people, Christians and non-Christians alike.**

Read **1 John 1:9**.
(4) What solution is given here for the problem of sin? _____

_____.

God has made it clear in Scripture that the only unforgiven sin is an unconfessed sin.

Read **Luke 18:9-14**.
(5) What do you see as the essential difference between the prayers of the two men? _____

_____.

(6) Which of the two men does Jesus say was forgiven? _____.
(7) Therefore, what must be our attitude when we come to God in prayer? _____.

Discussion Question: What is true humility?

Read **Matthew 23:14**.
(8) What does Jesus accuse the Pharisee of doing about his sins?

_____.

(9) Is Jesus condemning the idea of long prayers in general, or is he talking about an attitude of the heart? _____.

(10) What is this attitude? _____.

Read **1 Peter 3:7**.
(11) What does Peter call on men to do? _____.

(12) What does he say will happen if they don't do this? _____

_____.

Discussion Question: Why do you think God drew attention to this particular problem?

Although this passage is addressed to men, God is no respecter of persons, and what is required of husbands is also required of wives. All married people must be considerate of their mates.

Read **Daniel 10:12-13**.
(13) What was the reason for the delay given by the Archangel Michael? _____.

We are engaged in spiritual warfare and the enemy is as anxious to see that our prayers go unanswered as we are to have them answered.
(14) Summarize some of the reasons our prayers may not be

answered. _____
_____
_____.

Now that we have considered some of the reasons why our prayers go unanswered, let us take a long look at examples of answered prayer in the Bible and see if we can understand some of the principles involved.

Read **Acts 1:14.**
(15) What two qualities are mentioned in this verse? _____
_____.

The Amplified Bible gives us the additional information that they "devoted themselves steadfastly" to prayer.

Read **Acts 6:4.**
(16) Why did the disciples not want to be bothered with petty administrative problems? _____.

(17) Which subject did they put first? _____.
All too often, we put everything else in our life before prayer and, if we have time left or when all else fails, we pray. Following the Resurrection of Christ and Pentecost, we find that prayer has first priority with the disciples, as it did in the life of Jesus.

Discussion Question: Most of us are already too busy: how can we give prayer top priority in our lives?

Read **Matthew 14:23** and **Matthew 26:36.**

(18) What do we find Jesus doing in these two Scriptures? _____
_____.

These are only two of many examples of Jesus going apart to pray. Prayer (communication with His Father) was as essential to Him as eating and breathing.

Discussion Question: When is it right to "go apart" and when is it right to pray with others?

Read **James 5:16** (Amplified Bible).
(19) What three adjectives are used in this verse concerning prayer?
_____.

Read **Acts 12:5.**
(20) How was the church praying for Peter? _____.
Several other versions of the Bible describe the prayer going up for Peter as "earnest."

Read **Philippians 4:6** and **Colossians 4:2**.
(21) How are we advised to pray in these verses? _____.
Read **1 Corinthians 14:15**.
(22) How does Paul say he prays in this verse? _____
_____.

Read **Matthew 6:6-7**.
(23) What two suggestions for prayer does the Lord give? _____
_____.

In our culture, we do not generally pray in public, particularly on street corners as the Israelites once did, but perhaps on occasion we have put on a pose of prayer in church or elsewhere for the benefit of others. However most of us will have to plead guilty to the charge of "vain repetitions."

Read **Genesis 12:1-7, Genesis 15:1-4** and **Genesis 21:5**.
(24) Approximately how old was Abraham when God first promised him an heir? _____.

(25) How old was he when Isaac was born? _____.
(26) Sometimes our prayers are not immediately answered. If, however, we feel God has given us His word, then we must exercise _____.

Read **Luke 11:5-8**.
(27) According to this Scripture we must pray _____.
Read **Hebrews 4:16**.
(28) How does the author tell us to approach God? _____.
Read **John 14:13, John 15:16** and **John 16:24**.
(29) How did Jesus say to pray? _____.

Discussion Question: What did Jesus mean when He said to pray "in my name"?

(30) John 16:24 tells us the end result of praying in Jesus' name is what? _____.

Discussion Question: What are some of the things God gives you that bring you a fullness of joy?

In John 15:16, the asking and giving are connected with fruit.
Read **Galatians 5:22**.
(31) What would this fruit be? _____.
(32) In John 14:13, the asking and doing is in order that the Father may be _____.

Discussion Question: What situations could qualify for this?

In James 4:2, there is a description of how many people pray much of the time.
(33) What do they fail to do? _____.
Read **Matthew 7:7**.
(34) Here are three distinct planes of prayer. The first phrase says

_____.

This is the form of communication between God and a new Christian — asking, receiving. God doesn't want us to stay a little child, though, and maturity implies shouldering responsibility. This is

implied in the second phrase, _____. In the Scriptures, "seek" usually refers to seeking God. God wants to fellowship with us, on a deeper plane than we have experienced

before. The third phase has to do with _____.
We knock and a door is opened; when we go through the door, ministry is the result. Whatever we feel our ministry to be — teaching, hospitality, singing, evangelism, helps, etc., in order to be fruitful, we must ask God to open the doors for us. We must not set out in our own strength.

Impatience is part of our old man. Yet every Christian sooner or later must come to terms with the fact that God and man operate on different time tables. In this matter we must trust God. We know such a small part of the complete picture from God's point of view.
Read **Isaiah 5:18-19**.

(35) What does man want? _____.
We have saved two of the most important aspects of answered prayer for the last.

Read **Mark 11:24**.
(36) What adjective does this Scripture use with the word "things"?

_____.

(37) What is the condition Jesus gives for having our prayers

answered? _____.
Other versions of the Bible indicate a change in the verb tense of "receive." To have the faith necessary to have our prayers answered, we must believe that we have already received what we are praying for.
Read **Matthew 17:20**.
(38) What is the condition for answered prayer, given here? _____

_____.

Read **Matthew 17:14-20**.

(39) Why does Jesus say the disciples could not cast out the demon from the boy? _____.

Much has been written about the faith that Jesus talks about here and how much faith is enough faith to move mountains. Obviously, the disciples did not have that kind of faith at this point. We can be grateful that this kind of faith is not the **only** route to answered prayer. However, the Bible does show us ways to increase our faith. Read **Mark 9:17-24.**

Mark gives us some additional details concerning this same story.

(40) In verse 23, what does Jesus say to the father? _____.

(41) What is the father's response? _____.

Since the boy was healed, we must assume that Jesus answered the man's prayer for more faith.

(42) What is one way of receiving greater faith? _____.
Read **Romans 12:3.**
(43) How much faith is given to each of us? _____.

Discussion Question: Do you believe a measure of faith is sufficient to receive answers to our prayers? Why or why not?

Read **Romans 10:17.**
(44) According to this passage of Scripture, what is another way of increasing our faith? _____.
Read **James 1:12.**
(45) What is one other way our faith can be increased? (implied) _____.

Read **1 Corinthians 12:9.**
(46) What kind of faith is talked about here? _____.

When we do not have the faith necessary to have our prayers answered, we need to pray for more faith, immerse ourselves in Scripture so that our faith may grow.

There is yet one more thing to consider.
Read **1 John 5:14-15.**
(47) What must we look for now? _____.
Read **Romans 12:2.**
(48) Two important steps are given here. First we must not _____. Then we must _____

This whole verse speaks of a progression. Not being transformed to the world cannot be accomplished overnight. It is an on-going work of the Lord. As time goes by, we are less and less conformed to the world and we are more and more transformed by the renewing of our minds.

(49) What are the three steps listed here? _____

_____.

Again, a progression is indicated. First, we learn what is good; next we learn what is acceptable, and finally as mature Christians, we learn the perfect will of God.

Doing God's will is not easy. It frequently costs us something. It has cost some people their lives. Only one person ever completely did the will of the Father; that was Jesus, and doing His Father's will was not always easy, even for Him.

Read Matthew 26:36-46
Authorities are not in agreement as to exactly what the "cup" was that Jesus asked to be taken away, whether it was the death on the cross or some aspect of it. However, there is no room for disagreement as to how Jesus prayed or God's answer to His prayer.

(50) How many times did Jesus pray? _____.
(51) What did Jesus want more than a positive answer to His prayer?

_____.

Read **Luke 22:39-45**.
Luke's account of the same event gives us additional details.

(52) What was Jesus' emotional state? _____.

(53) What did God send Him? _____.

Jesus basically prayed the same prayer three times. Notice that as soon as He had finished His prayer, the actions which led to His crucifixion began.

(54) How did God answer Jesus' prayer? _____.

Too often as Christians, when God's answer to our prayer is a "no," we say God did not answer that prayer. It is always important to remember that God has three answers to our prayers: "yes," "no" and "wait."

Discussion Question: What would have happened if God had said "Yes" to Jesus prayer?

The purpose of all our prayer should not be to change God's mind, but rather to **discern His perfect will in the matter at hand and bring our will into submission to His.**

Personal Application
(1) Do I give prayer its proper place in my life?
(2) Have I considered my prayers from a concerned Father's point of view? How many of my prayers would have been harmful to me if God had answered "yes" to them?
(3) When I pray, which is more important to me — receiving what I ask for or being in the Lord's will?

Notebook Assignment
Look over your list of prayer requests in your notebook. In the light of what you believe (know) to be God's will for you, are there any you should delete? If so, cross them out as a matter of obedience.

Are there any areas of your life where having your own way is more important to you than seeking, accepting or following God's will? Write these down. Be scrupulously honest here. If you can, give these areas to God, ask His forgiveness and make it a matter of your will to put God's will for you first. If you can't take this step now, ask God to bring you to the point where you will be willing.

Advanced Study
Read **Numbers 11.**
(1) What does God sometimes do when we complain too much? Can you find any other instances in the Bible in which the Lord answered someone's prayer to his regret?
(2) Learn as much as you can about what the Bible specifically says is the will of God for your life.

Enrichment Assignment for Chapter 4.
(1) Make a study of all the tithes and offerings the Lord required of the Israelites.
(2) Read the story of Jesus' healing ministry in the Gospel of Luke. Come to a decision as to God's attitude toward illness of all kinds.

Memory Work
(1) "So faith comes from hearing, and hearing by the word of Christ" (Romans 10:17).
(2) "Jesus said to him, 'If you can! All things are possible to him who believes'" (Mark 9:23).
(3) "Confess your sins to one another, and pray for one another, so that you may be healed" (James 5:16).

Lesson Four

What Can We Pray For?

Introduction

Too few Christians are aware of the storehouse of information in the Bible concerning what we should and may pray for. Frequently we vacillate between two camps. On the one hand, we hesitate to make a move without asking God; on the other, we turn to Him only in the direst of emergencies.

Prayer: Oh, Father, how often have we prayed amiss because we have not sought Your will. Today, we truly seek it. Teach us what you want us to know. Amen.

Discussion Question: What has God shown you this past week, as you have been obedient to His will?

Bible Study

In the Lord's Prayer, the Lord provides us with a good outline on which we can, to a large degree, base our prayer life.
Read **Luke 11:2-4** and **Matthew 6:9-13.**
(1) Specifically, what six areas did Jesus instruct his disciples to pray for?

    a. Hallowed (glorify) _____.

    b. Thy _____.

    c. Give us _____.

    d. Forgive _____.

    e. Lead _____.

    f. Deliver _____.

The first two points are concerned with our relationship with God and the establishing of His kingdom on earth. As in the Ten Commandments God commands us to get our priorities in the right order. Only as we put God first will the rest of our life fall into place.

Our daily bread represents all of our material needs.

(2) According to the Lord's Prayer are we scriptural then in praying for our material needs? _____.

Discussion Question: Why do you think the Lord told us to pray for them on a daily basis?

Read **Matthew 6:25-33.**

(3) What does Jesus tell us not to be anxious about?_____
_____.

(4) Does this mean we should not pray for these things?_____.
Jesus is speaking here of a preoccupation, a real concern or worry about our minimum material needs. It is natural to worry about such things, particularly if we are the breadwinner or if we are in charge of balancing the budget. But, as children of the King, we are not limited to doing the natural thing.

(5) What is our first priority according to verse 33? _____
_____.

(6) What is the promise attached to this condition? _____
_____.

Discussion Question: How do we put the Kingdom of God and His righteousness first?

George Mueller, in providing for his orphans, daily put this verse to the test. If our cupboard is bare, but we are putting the Kingdom of God first, then we needn't worry. God has promised to feed us. This may come through the church, a job, friends, or many different ways, but we will not go hungry.

Read **Romans 14:17.**

(7) What are three attributes of the Kingdom of God? _____
_____.

We have already discussed forgiveness in the previous chapter, so we will not spend more time on it here. Part of Question 1, concerns itself with temptation. We are surrounded by temptations, but God has given us His word on one aspect of it.

Read **James 1:14.**

(8) Why are we tempted?_____.

Read **1 Corinthians 10:13.**

(9) What is our defense against temptation? _____
_____.

Desire for more and more material possessions is a frequent and constant temptation for many Christians.

Discussion Question: In an affluent society how much more are we allowed to have than our daily bread?

(10) What risk do we always run when we have too many material possessions? _____.

Read **Matthew 6:24.**
(11) What does Jesus say about lusting after material things? _____
_____.

Coupled with the desire for material possessions can be the desire for power and position. This was one of the temptations Satan tempted Jesus with in the wilderness.

Read **Luke 4:5-8.**
(12) What was Jesus' response to Satan? _____
_____.

Many Christians continually live in a state of virtual poverty or below a decent standard of living. They have prayed and prayed for financial blessings and still they have seen no visible response to their prayers. This may very well be because God has provided another and a better way to lead us to financial prosperity. His way is both better for us and better for the Kingdom.

Read **Malachi 3:8-11.**
(13) What are we told we must do? _____
_____.

(14) What happens when we are obedient? _____
_____.

(15) What does God say about those who "rob" him of the tithes and offerings?_____.

The Scriptural definition of the tithe is 10% of one's income (cf. Leviticus 27:30-32). Your offerings are in addition to that.

Discussion Question: What do you think the storehouse is?

Most Christian authorities agree that the storehouse is your local church, the place where you are consistently fed. This is where your tithe goes. After prayer, you will be led by the Lord as to where your offerings should go.

Read **Proverbs 11:24-25.**
(16) What do these verses say happens to those who give generously?

(17) What is the fate of those who are selfish and keep everything they have for themselves? _____.

Read **Proverbs 28:27** and **Proverbs 19:17**.
(18) What quality in His people does God love? _____.

(19) Special blessings are also given in connection with what? _____.

Read **Luke 6:38** and **2 Corinthians 9:6**.
(20) These verses tell us we receive in proportion to _____.

When we give, we bless the Kingdom of God and we are blessed by God in return. Before we pray about our material needs, we must make sure we are meeting God's other requirements.

Jesus also taught us to pray, "Deliver us from evil."

One of the evils of all times has been physical illness and handicaps. We do not need to read far in the Gospels to learn God's attitude toward illness. When Jesus lived on earth, despite His attempts to down play the healing aspect of His ministry, much of His fame was due to it.

Read **Matthew 8:16-17**.
(21) Who were healed in these verses? _____.

The name spoken of as "Esaias" in some versions of the Bible is Isaiah.

Read **Isaiah 53:5**.
(22) What does this passage tell us? _____.

In the Jerusalem Bible, this passage is translated as, "Yet He was pierced through for our faults, crushed for our sins. On Him lies a punishment that brings us peace and through His wounds we are healed."

Just as there are conditions attached to the acquiring of financial prosperity, there is also one important condition related to claiming this promise for physical health.

Read **Exodus 23:25**.
(23) What is our role in receiving health? _____.

The Bible also gives us many other guidelines related to what we should be praying for.

Read **Matthew 5:44-45**.
(24) Who are we supposed to pray for? _____.

(25) Why? _____.
Read **1 Timothy 2:1-4**.
(26) Who do these verses tell us to pray for? _____.

God is vitally interested in good government. When there is no tyranny, then Christians have free rein to witness and to spread the Gospel.

Discussion Question: What would happen if all Christians ardently prayed for their country?

Read **2 Peter 3:9**.
(27) What does this verse tell us about God's will? _____
_____.

(28) Therefore, we can always pray for whom, knowing we are in God's will? _____.

Read **Proverbs 22:6**.
(29) This verse tells us that God is interested in whom?_____.

He has promised that if we train our children properly to fear the Lord and to love their neighbors, when they are old, they will abide by these teachings. Therefore, if our children temporarily stray away, it is God's will for us to pray for them in faith, with authority, to bring them back speedily.

Read **James 1:5-8**.
(30) When faced with decisions, many of us have trouble discerning the better course of action. What has God promised to give us?
_____.

(31) How are we supposed to pray? _____.

Read **Deuteronomy 31:8** and **Psalm 121:4**.

Many of us have fears — fears of the dark, of famine and war, poverty, fear for our children's safety, a fear of strangers of unfamiliar situations.

(32) What has the Lord promised? _____
_____
_____.

Here is solid assurance for any situation we may fear.

Read **Psalm 147:3**
(33) Who does God promise to heal? _____.

If circumstances or people have shattered our life, God will bind us up and heal us if we ask Him to.

(34) A concise list of God's promises will help us to know which petitions are acceptable. Using answers you have already written down, fill in the blanks below. We may pray for

   a. Deuteronomy 31:8 _____.

   b. Psalm 147:3 _____.

   c. Proverbs 22:6_____.

   d. Isaiah 53:5 _____.

   e. Matthew 5:44-45 _____.

   f. Matthew 8:16-17 _____.

   g. 1 Timothy 2:1-4_____.

   h. James 1:5 _____.

   i. 2 Peter 3:9 _____.

Read **Luke 11:9-13.**

(35) What do these verses have to say about getting our prayers answered? _____.

(36) How does Jesus portray the Father in these verses?_____.

(37) Does He indicate there is anything we should not pray for? ____.

Once we have established that we are praying in God's will and when we have met the conditions of answered prayer, we can come to the throne of God with boldness, trusting Him to answer our prayer in a way that is most beneficial to us and to His kingdom.

Personal Application

(1) Does the Kingdom of God have top priority in my life?
(2) Most answered prayer comes as a result of our doing our part and God doing His. Do I always make sure I have done my part before I ask God to do His?
(3) Do I have "hang-ups" about God, or do I always see Him as a loving Father, anxious to answer my prayers?

Notebook Assignment

If you are not presently tithing, see if you can convince your family (or if you are single, make your decision) that the tithe is the basis of a

Scriptural principle. Begin a six-month experiment and see if you are not blessed financially by your obedience. Keep strict records of your giving and your receiving. Always take your tithe off the top; if you wait to see if there is enough money left over at the end of the week or month, there usually won't be.

If you are already a tither, begin to make offerings above the tithe. Many Christians today are trying to give a second tithe for missionary work, etc. Keep a record in your notebook of all giving and receiving.

If giving generously is a firmly established pattern in your life, take a look at your attitudes. We can be legalists as far as giving money is concerned and yet not have a truly giving nature. Perhaps we have a part of ourselves we refuse to share with others. Seek the Lord on this matter and see if He reveals any areas of selfishness in your life. With His help, make it a matter of will to become a more generous and sharing person. Record your experiences in your notebook.

Advanced Studies

(1) Make a complete study of all the physical healings performed by Jesus in the Gospels.
(2) Make a study of everything related in the New Testament about the Kingdom of God (Kingdom of Heaven).
(3) Look up other promises God makes for the children of Christians.

Enrichment Assignment for Chapter 5

(1) Read **John 7:39** and answer these questions: a. Why is "speaking in tongues" not part of Old Testament worship? b. Did Jesus speak in tongues?
(2) Study the Jewish Festival of Pentecost.

Memory Work

(1) "Surely our griefs He Himself bore and our sorrows He carried; yet we ourselves esteemed Him stricken, smitten of God, and afflicted. But He was pierced through for our transgressions, He was crushed for our iniquities; the chastening for our well-being fell upon Him; and by His scourging we are healed" (Isa. 53:4-5).
(2) "Give, and it will be given to you; good measure, pressed down, shaken together, running over, they will pour into your lap. For by your standard of measure it will be measured to you in return" (Luke 6:38).
(3) "If any of you lacks wisdom, let him ask of God, who gives to all men generously and without reproach, and it will be given to him" (James 1:5).

Lesson Five

Praying in the Spirit

Introduction

For many Christians who are baptized in the Holy Spirit, praying in the Holy Spirit is as natural and as necessary as eating and drinking. However, for others, praying in the Spirit is an unfamiliar idea. Let's explore the topic in the best journalistic tradition, answering the questions: What? Who? How? When? Where? and Why?

Prayer: Father, today we may be learning something of Your ways that is new to many of us. Give us open minds to receive. And if this is not new to others, then give us a deeper level of understanding. Amen.

Discussion Question: Share your tithing, offering or giving experiences with the group.

Bible Study

Read **1 Corinthians 14:2.**
(1) What is another phrase for "praying in the Spirit"? _____

_____.

Speaking in the Spirit may not always mean speaking in tongues. It may also indicate the beautiful communion you sometimes feel with God when no words at all are spoken. However, for purposes of this study, we will regard speaking in the Spirit as being the same as speaking in tongues.

Read **Acts 2:1-5.**
Pentecost is considered the birth of the Christian Church and is an important feast day in the liturgical churches.

(2) On what Jewish holiday did this event take place? _____.

(3) Who was meeting that day? _____.

(4) What happened to them? _____.

(5) Who gave the believers this ability? _____.

(6) Who received this blessing? _____.

Read **Acts 2:6-11.**
(7) What made the people outside come running? _____

_____.

(8) What was their reaction upon hearing the believers speak? ____

_____.

(9) How many different languages are mentioned? _____.

(10) In this instance, the "tongues" were _____.

God used these different known languages as a witness to unbelievers, just as He has in many documented cases all over the world today.

Read **Acts 2:14-18.**
(11) What Old Testament prophet did Peter quote? _____.

(12) Summarize the quotation. _____

_____.

The men present were all Jews from many different countries. They would all have been familiar with the passage Peter recited.

Read **Acts 2:37.**
(13) What effect did Peter's speech have on his listeners? _____

_____.

Read **Acts 2:38.**
(14) What did Peter instruct them to do? _____

_____.

(15) What did he tell them they would receive? _____

_____.

Read **Acts 2:41.**
(16) How many souls were saved that day? _____.

Read **1 Corinthians 13:1**
(17) What two kinds of "tongues" are mentioned here? _____

_____.

The tongues of men is undoubtedly a known language, while the tongues of angels would refer to an unknown language, created by God for a specific believer's use.

Read **Acts 2:39.**
(18) What is the promise referred to here? _____.

(19) What three groups of people is the promise for? _____

_____.

(20) Does that include you? _____.

Scripture shows us that it is a normal and expected step for a believer to receive the baptism of the Holy Spirit.

Read **Acts 8:9-17.**

The baptism of the Holy Spirit was not reserved for the day of Pentecost. Four other separate accounts of people receiving this baptism after Pentecost are given in the New Testament.

(21) Who received the baptism of the Holy Spirit in this instance?

_____.

Read **Acts 9:1-7; 1 Corinthians 14:18.**
(22) Who received in this case? _____.

Read **Acts 10:23-24, 44-48.**
(23) Who were the recipients? _____.

Read **Acts 19:1-6.**
(24) Who received it in this instance? _____.

Please note that while the baptism of the Holy Spirit was received with the laying on of hands in three cases, this was not true in the other one. God will not be boxed in; His ways and methods are infinite, and we, too, must not be bound by one given method that has been used in the past.

Discussion Question: Must a person speak in tongues when she receives the baptism of the Holy Spirit? Why or why not?

Read **Acts 10:44-46.**
(25) These verses say that tongues were taken as a sign that _____

_____.

Read **Acts 2:4.**
(26) Three definite steps in speaking in another language are given

here. They were all _____.

Then they began _____ as the Spirit _____

_____. Just as you must take the first step in drawing near to God before He will draw near to you, so you must take the first steps in speaking in tongues. You ask for the Holy Spirit. God gives it to you. You open your mouth to make a sound; the Spirit forms that sound into words.

There are two distinct manifestations of speaking in tongues. At Pentecost, the group in the Upper Room all received known languages which the Jews understood. Frequently, those baptized in the Holy Spirit do not receive a known tongue for their prayer language.

(27) The second speaking in tongues is called the **gift** of _____.
Read **1 Corinthians 14:13-14.**
(28) What should this always be accompanied by? _____.

Discussion Question: How do you receive the other gifts?

Although this verse has been used as an argument against speaking in tongues, Paul was actually warning against the excessive use of the gift of tongues at a public meeting.

Discussion Question: Is speaking in tongues for everyone?

Since speaking in tongues is sometimes the cause of controversy in the church today, why should we seek this gift from God?
Read **John 16:7-14.**
(29) Why did Jesus say it was expedient that He go away? _____

_____.

(30) List all the things Jesus said the Holy Spirit would do when He

came? _____

_____

_____.

Since Jesus regards the Holy Spirit so highly, doesn't it behoove each of us to have as much of Him as we possibly can?
Read **Luke 24:49.**
(31) What was Jesus' final command to His followers? _____

_____.

(32) What did Jesus say His followers would receive along with the

promise? _____.
·Compare **John 21** with **Acts 2 and 3.**
(33) What is the striking difference in Peter in these chapters? _____

_____.

Compare **Luke 9:37-40** to **Acts 3:1-8.**
(34) What is the outstanding difference in the ability of the disciples

as recorded in these two portions of Scripture? _____

_____.

We need only compare Peter's behavior at Jesus' arrest and his death as a martyr many years later to realize that something very important happened to him on the day of Pentecost, something which changed him from a coward who denied His Lord to a martyr that tradition tells us requested to be crucified upside down because he felt he was not worthy to die the same death as his Lord.

When we receive the baptism in the Holy Spirit, we receive power, to be self-life losers and the power necessary to witness for the Lord and to live our lives in Him in these days of increasing darkness.
Read **Romans 8:26-27.**
We have all faced situations in which we were not sure of the will of God. Consequently, we really didn't know how to pray or what to ask for. This is our weakness, our infirmity, because we don't know the perfect will of Christ.

Discussion Question: What are some of the situations in your life for which you don't know God's will?

(35) What happens when we pray in the Spirit? _____

_____.

Read **Ephesians 6:10-18.**
(36) What is to accompany the taking up of the full armor of God?

(v. 18) _____.
All Christians whether they are aware of it or not are engaged in a spiritual war. Praying in the Spirit is a vital piece of armor.
Read **Jude 20.**
(37) What does Paul say happens when you pray in the Spirit? _____

_____.

Read **1 Corinthians 14:2.**
(38) Although the main thrust of this verse is to diminish the misuse of tongues in the Corinthian church, Paul says that when we

pray in tongues we speak _____.
Read **1 Corinthians 14:4.**
(39) What does the speaking of tongues do to the speaker? _____.
Read **1 Corinthians 14:18.**
(40) What is Paul's attitude toward the speaking in tongues? _____

_____.

Read **1 Corinthians 14:14.**
(41) What happens to your mind when you pray in tongues? _____

_____.

At first glance, this passage might seem to belittle tongues. But what is it that stands in the way of prayer? Understanding!

When we pray in our native language, there are many handicaps. We are bound by the limitations of our knowledge of the situation from God's point of view; we are limited by our vocabulary. Then any distraction at all, including the distraction of our thoughts, gets in the way and we frequently come away from our prayer time frustrated. However, when we pray in the Spirit, all these handicaps are overcome. The Spirit of God Himself prays through us, as we surrender

our tongues and whole speech area to Him. It is not our knowledge that guides the prayer; it is not our vocabulary; distractions come and go, but we continue praying in the Spirit without interruption.
Read **1 Corinthians 14:15.**
(42) Should we pray only in the Spirit? _____.

Personal Application

(1) Have I resisted receiving the baptism of the Holy Spirit, allowing myself to be satisfied with less than God wants to give me?
(2) Do I pray in the Spirit daily or is my heavenly language reserved for "special occasions and emergencies"?
(3) Do I use my tongues as a language of praise and worship to the Lord?

Notebook Assignment

As an act of discipline, pray in tongues for a specific time daily for a set time, e.g. a month. Record your observations after a few days and throughout the month: Do you feel any different? Are you edified when you pray? Has your relationship to God changed in any way? Etc.

Be open for God to use you in one or more of the other spiritual gifts during your worship time at your Bible study. This is a good place for you to practice if you have a tendency to hold back. If you are already experienced in the gifts, then wait for one of the more reticent members to speak out. Record your feelings in your notebook, whether you spoke out or waited for another one to speak.

Advanced Studies

(1) Make a study of the other gifts of the Spirit.
(2) How are the other gifts related to speaking in tongues?

Enrichment Assignment for Chapter 6

(1) Make a list of all the reasons you personally should be offering praise and thanksgiving to the Lord.

Memory Work

(1) "And it will come about after this that I will pour out My Spirit upon all mankind; and your sons and daughters will prophesy, your old men will dream dreams, your young men will see visions. And even on the male and female servants I will pour out My Spirit in those days" (Joel 2:28-29).
(2) "And they were all filled with the Holy Spirit and began to speak with other tongues, as the Spirit was giving them utterance" (Acts 2:4).
(3) "And when Paul had laid his hands upon them, the Holy Spirit came on them; and they began speaking with tongues, and prophesying" (Acts 19:6).

Lesson Six

Praise and Thanksgiving

Introduction

"Shout joyfully to God, all the earth!"
"I will give thanks to the Lord with all my heart."
"Bless the Lord, O my soul."
"Praise the Lord! Oh give thanks to the Lord."
"Praise the Lord, all nations; laud Him, all people."

Over and over in Scripture, we are told to praise God, to thank Him, to bless Him, to worship Him, to lift up His Name. Scripture commands us 555 times just to praise and worship the Lord.

Why? Is it because God needs our praises, our recognition? Is His self-image dependent on a worshipping, adoring people? Does His ego need feeding?

Of course not! Although our praises do give Him pleasure, God doesn't need them in the sense that He is incomplete without them. Rather, we have been exhorted to praise and worship the Lord, to be grateful to Him because we need a center outside ourselves. This is the way He has made us.

Prayer: Father, so often we have come to You with only our selfish requests. Today, teach us to know You as a God who deserves our praise and thanksgiving. Amen.

Discussion Question: What happened as you prayed in tongues this past week?

Bible Study

Discussion Question: What qualities in man make worshipping God essential to his well being?

Read **Psalm 103:8.**

The first thing we must settle in our hearts once and for all is that God is entirely worthy of our praise and worship.

(1) In verse 8, what four attributes of the Lord are given? _____

_____.

Read **Psalm 103:1-14.**

(2) Many other attributes are also implied by His actions. For instance, in Verse 3, the fact that He forgives all our iniquities means that He is forgiving. What other attribute is implied in verse 3? _____.

(3) What three qualities are referred to in verse 4? _____
_____.

(4) What quality in verse 5? _____.

(5) What two qualities in verse 6? _____.

(6) What quality in verse 13? _____.

(7) In verse 14? _____.

Read **Isaiah 40:9-28.**

(8) In this chapter Isaiah describes the magnificence of God. Different verses deal with different aspects. For instance, Verse 10 is concerned with strength. What other aspects are described?

Verse 11 _____.

Verse 12 _____.

Verses 13-14 _____.

Verses 15, 16, 17, 22, 23_____.

Verse 26_____and_____.

Verse 27 _____.

Verse 28_____and_____.

When we truly begin to catch a glimpse of who God is and what He is truly like, our natural response should be one of worship and adoration. We must always remember that God does not just **have** these qualities, He is these qualities. He is not only merciful; He is mercy. There is no true concept of the quality known as mercy apart from God. This is true of all His attributes.

We worship and praise the Lord for who and what He is; we are grateful and thankful for what He has done for us.

Read **Isaiah 61:1-3** and **Luke 4:16-21.** (See KJV also).

(9) The prophet, explaining that the Spirit of the Lord God was upon him, prophesied here the work of Jesus. When Jesus read this Scripture in the synogogue, He did not read all of verse 2. When will the day of vengeance take place? _____.

(10) What has God done for us in verse 1? _____

_____

_____.

(11) Verse 3? _____

_____.

Beauty would be a garland of flowers to wear instead of the ashes the Hebrews traditionally daubed on themselves when mourning. The spirit of heaviness is despondency or depression. Depression is truly lifted when we realize God is able to do all things and that He cares about us. It is almost impossible to stay "down in the dumps" after praising the Lord for a time.

Read **Psalm 147.**

(12) In these verses over 20 things the Lord has done and is doing for us are mentioned. Make a list of those for which you are personally grateful. Perhaps on another sheet of paper you might want to list all that you can find. The Psalm lists many attributes of God as well.

_____

_____

_____

_____.

Read **2 Chronicles 20:14-25.**

Praise has frequently been used as a spiritual weapon by the children of God. These verses tell the story of what happened when King Jehoshaphat, the King of Judah, was attacked by a mighty army. Jehoshaphat called for a fast throughout all Judah; then he prayed mightily to the Lord.

(13) When the Lord's answer came, what did Jehoshaphat and his troops do on the day of battle? _____.

(14) What did the Lord do while they were praising and worshipping?

_____.

(15) What were the final results of that day's warfare? _____

_____

_____.

In these days of great spiritual attack and warfare, we must remember that praise is one of our greatest weapons.

Discussion Question: What similarities do you see between this story and that of Joshua at Jericho?

Read **Psalm 22:3**.

Are you beginning to see a connection between the actions of God and your praising? If so, you are on the right track.

(16) This Psalm tells us that God _____ our praises.

Read **1 Thessalonians 5:16-18**.

Praise knows no season; it is required of us regardless of our circumstances.

(17) How are we told to give thanks in these verses? _____
_____.

This does not mean that we are to thank and praise the Lord for our misfortunes and problems. However, we are commanded to thank the Lord and praise Him in the middle of these circumstances.

Read **Romans 8:28**.

(18) Why are we able to thank and praise the Lord in the middle of

completely unsurmountable problems? _____
_____.

Discussion Question: Can you think of any uncomfortable situations you are presently in, in which you need to give praise?

Read **Hebrews 13:15**.

Our praise of the Lord should not depend upon our mood. There will always be times when we just don't feel like praising Him; we have nothing good to say about anyone, or we're just too depressed to make the effort. God does not excuse us at times like these because He has given us the solution to our problem in the act of praise.

(19) When we are really "down" what kind of praise is required of

us? _____.

Perhaps because the Lord was aware of the very human characteristic of getting into ruts, He designed many different varieties of praise and ways to praise Him. If this is your first venture into a study of praise, you may be in for some surprises.

(20) What forms of praise are considered in the following verses:

Psalms 33:8 and 135:1-2? (standing) _____
_____.

Psalm 47:6 and Judges 5:2-3? _____.

Psalms 63:4, 134:2, 141:2? _____.

Acts 2:11, Acts 10:46? _____.

1 Corinthians 14:15 and Ephesians 5:18-19? _____.

Psalm 150? _____.

Joshua 6:10, 16, 20; Psalm 47:1? _____
_____.

2 Samuel 6:14; Psalm 150:4, Psalm 149:3? _____.

Psalm 126:2, Job 8:21? _____.

Luke 7:38? _____.

Psalm 46:10 (KJV)? _____.

Psalm 95:6, Luke 22:41? _____
_____.

Luke 17:16 and Revelation 4:10-11? _____
_____.

Discussion Question: Are there any of these ways of praising the Lord that you are reluctant to do?

Sometimes although we sincerely want to praise the Lord we are held back by factors either within us or without. It is necessary to recognize and deal with these problems before we can truly praise the Lord.

Read **Revelation 12:9, Job 1:6-12.**
(21) Who/what is at work in these verses? _____

One of Satan's most successful attacks against a person is when he successfully keeps her from praising.

Read **Psalm 66:18, Isaiah 59:2** and **1 John 1:9.**
(22) What is the problem revealed in these verses? _____
_____.

Sin separates us from the presence of God.

(23) How do we handle the sin in our lives? _____
_____.

Read **2 Timothy 1:7** and **1 John 4:18.**
(24) What common human failing is mentioned in these verses? ____

Read **Luke 19:21.**
(25) How does the man in this parable see his Master (representative of God)? _____

(26) How do we need to see God? _____

If we see God as harsh, tyrannical, exacting, unfeeling or austere, it is difficult to release praise to Him. We must always remind ourselves that Jesus was God come in the flesh and the characteristics He revealed on earth are the characteristics of God.

To come into the true spirit of praise and worship of God is not accomplished in a few moments time. In this hurry-skurry world it is important to set aside a time daily when we can sit quietly, apart from all distractions and come to know the Lord. In your household, this may mean getting up a bit earlier in the morning or staying up later at night. However you manage to do this, you will find it to be one of the most important aspects of your life in Christ.

Personal Application

(1) What are some of the things in my life that keep me from adequately praising the Lord?
(2) Do I really consider Him worthy of my praise?
(3) Do I take time daily to praise and thank Him just as I take time for other kinds of prayer?

Notebook Assignment

Many people have found a new sense of freedom and joy as they become freer in their worship of the Lord.

Choose one form of praise that you have never used before and use it every day for at least a month. Record your feelings in the diary section of your notebook.

List any negative or harsh qualities you have attributed to the Lord. Confess these to Him and ask His forgiveness. Several times a day, specifically praise Him for a positive quality that is opposite to the one you confessed. Do this for several months if necessary and record any differences in your attitude toward the Lord.

Advanced Study

(1) Search your Bible for other instances in which God fought the battle while His people praised Him.
(2) Make a study of the essential differences between praise and worship.

Enrichment Assignment for Chapter 7

(1) Research appearances of the Lord or "the Angel of the Lord" in Scripture.

(2) Study examples of intercessory prayer in the Bible and the outcome of each instance.
(3) Make a detailed study of Moses as an intercessor.

Memory Work

(1) "I will bless the Lord at all times; His praise shall continually be in my mouth. My soul shall make its boast in the Lord: The humble shall hear it, and rejoice" (Ps. 34:1).
(2) "Enter His gates with thanksgiving, and His courts with praise; give thanks to Him: bless His name" (Ps. 100:4).
(3) "Bless the Lord, O my soul; and all that is within me, bless His holy name. Bless the Lord, O my soul, and forget none of His benefits" (Ps. 103:1-2).

Lesson Seven
Intercessory Prayer

Introduction

The Bible repeatedly urges us to pray for one another, to pray for our families, our nation, fellow Christians and even the unsaved. But even apart from these admonitions of the Lord, there seems to be some innate quality in the heart of God's people that makes us want to make intercessions for those we love.

Time and time again the hand of God has been moved by the prayers of faithful intercessors, both in individual lives and the lives of nations.

Prayer: Lord, we have too often concerned ourselves with those close to us, our selves, our families, our friends. Open our hearts, so we may begin to see ourselves as members of the whole family of God. Amen.

Discussion Question: Share with your group the new form of praise you chose.

Bible Study

In the Old Testament, Moses is our example of the faithful intercessor, whose prayers for the Children of Israel saved them from the destructive and deadly fruit of their own sinful lives and actions.
Read **Exodus 24:12-18**.
(1)   Where was Moses at this time? _____.
Read **Exodus 32:1-6**.
(2)   What was the Israelites' excuse for what they did? _____
_____.
Read **Exodus 32:9-10**.
(3)   What did God say He would do to the Children of Israel? _____
_____.
Read **Exodus 32:11-14**.
(4)   What was Moses' plea for the Israelites? _____

(5) What was the Lord's response to Moses' entreaty? _____

_____

Discussion Question: Do you think God really intended to destroy the Israelites at this point or was He testing Moses' commitment to them?

Read **Deuteronomy 9.**
(6) In this chapter, Moses reveals some of the times he has interceded

for the Children of Israel. List them. _____

_____

_____

Discussion Question: Do you think the fact that the Children of Israel were afraid to hear from God directly had anything to do with their frequent sinning? (cp. Exodus 19:18-20).

Read **Nehemiah 1.**
(7) Who is Nehemiah interceding for? _____.

Read **Luke 2:37-38.**
(8) Who has Anna interceded for? _____.

Discussion Question: What qualities of character do these verses reveal about Anna?

Read **Luke 22:32.**
(9) What had Jesus prayed for Peter? _____.

Read **Philippians 1:9.**
(10) Who has Paul prayed for? _____.

Read **John 17.**
This prayer of Jesus has been called His High Priestly prayer. In the first part of the prayer, Jesus prays for Himself and the glory of the Father.
(11) What two other groups does Jesus pray for? _____

_____

If we are Christians today, we are the fruit of this prayer Jesus prayed almost 2,000 years ago.

Read **Hebrews 7:25.**
(12) What does this verse tell us Jesus is doing today? _____.

Read **Romans 8:26.**
(13) Who else is interceding for us? _____.

Isn't that wonderful? At this very moment we can rest in the knowledge that both Jesus and the Holy Spirit are making intercession for us.

One of the "prayingest" men in the Bible was Daniel. His prayers, reinforced by a sanctified life, kept God's protection over the Children of Israel during 70 years of exile from their own country and captivity in Babylon. In exchange, God did some amazing things for Daniel! By studying this man, we can catch a glimpse of the power of intercessory prayer and gain a deeper understanding of the importance of frequent, regular, earnest prayer on the behalf of others.

After the death of King Solomon in 931 B.C. the Hebrew nation split into two kingdoms, Israel and Judah, each occupying separate areas and each having its own kings. Most of these kings worshipped idols and generally "did what was wrong in the eyes of the Lord." For 200 years, God sent prophets to warn them to change their ways — Amos, Hosea, Micah — but the people refused to pay attention. Finally, God's patience wore thin and in 721 B.C., Israel was captured by Assyria, and in 587 B.C., Judah was occupied by the Babylonains. The Hebrews who didn't escape to Egypt were deported to Babylon as slaves, and the temple and all the city of Jerusalem were destroyed.

But these were God's Chosen People, and even though they had turned their backs on Him He didn't desert them.

Read **Daniel 1:1-18.**

(14) Under what circumstances were Daniel, Shadrach, Meshack and Abednego set apart? _____

_____

_____

(15) What did Daniel suggest? _____

_____

Discussion Question: When we are asked to do something which we believe is wrong what other alternatives besides out-and-out refusal are available to us?

(16) What are the result of Daniel's suggestion? _____

_____

The Babylonian Empire spread over more territory and encompassed more people than any other empire ever had up to that time. So Daniel and his friends were at the mercy of an absolute monarch whose word was literally law. His own homeland destroyed, Daniel lived in a city of highly skilled artisans, military men and engineers.

Read **Daniel 1:19-21.**

(17) How did Nebuchadnezzar feel about these young men? _____

_____

Discussion Question: Are Christians today known for their wisdom and understanding? Why or why not?

Read **Daniel 2:1-9.**
(18) Why was Nebuchadnezzar troubled? _____

_____.

(19) What did he demand of his magicians? _____.

(20) What was their response (v. 10)? _____

_____.

Read **Daniel 2:10-45.**
(21) What was Daniel's response to the men who came to kill him?

_____.

Note the serenity of his question to the captain of the king's bodyguard. Daniel did not waste time pleading his innocence or crying over the unfairness of the king's decree.
(22) What did Daniel do before he prayed? _____

_____.

Discussion Question: By asking for his friends' prayers, what New Testament principle was Daniel applying?

(23) What did God do for Daniel?_____

_____.

Read **Daniel 2:46-49.**
(24) What did the king say about Daniel's God? _____

_____.

(25) What promotion did Daniel receive?_____

_____.

(26) What did he get permission to do?_____

_____.

Daniel was well aware of his role as an intercessor. He quickly asked for permission to delegate the new responsibility which would have required him to leave the court. He knew that God wanted him to be right at court where he could have the greatest influence on King Nebuchadnezzar, watching over the interest of his captive nation.

While King Nebuchadnezzar believed the God of Daniel was "the God of gods," he did not believe He was the one true God.

Read **Daniel 3:1-13.**
(27) What did Nebuchadnezzar do? _____.

(28) What did the edict say? _____.

(29) How did Shadrach, Meshack and Abednego respond to the king's edict? _____
_____.

Read **Daniel 3:13-18.**
(30) What did the three men say when they were accused? _____
_____.

Read **Daniel 3:19-27.**
(31) What happened to them in the furnace? _____
_____.

Discussion Question: When can we expect God to intervene supernaturally in our situations?

Read **Daniel 3:28-30.**
(32) What was the king's response to the miracle? _____
_____.

Read **Daniel 4.**
(33) How does the Lord humble Nebuchadnezzar? _____
_____.

(34) At the end of the chapter how did Nebuchadnezzar honor God?
_____.

Discussion Question: Which kind of experiences, pleasant or unpleasant, are more likely to give us a revelation of God's glory.

Read **Daniel 5.**
(35) Chapter 5 is the story of the "handwriting on the wall." In spite of the unfavorable interpretation, Belshazzar accepted it and kept his word and _____ Daniel. Fortunately, Belshazzar acted immediately because he wasn't around the next day.

Read **Daniel 6.**
(36) Why was Daniel thrown into the pit of lions? _____
_____.

(37) Why was he not harmed? _____.

(38) What was the king's attitude (vss. 18-23) _____
_____.

Read **Daniel 9.**
(39) How does Daniel realize that the time for the end of the Jews'

captivity was at hand? _____.

(40) What was his response? _____.

(41) What happened as a result of his response? _____
_____.

Daniel is a tremendous example of faith in action. For 70 years he stood almost single-handed between the most mighty empire in the world and the Hebrew people. And while the Hebrews were indeed captured or scattered, they were not utterly destroyed. Daniel's influence over a succession of seven kings kept them safe. And when Daniel's life itself was endangered, God intervened with miracles.

Read **Daniel 6:10.**
(42) Where did Daniel get his faith, his peace of mind? _____
_____.

Discussion Question: If this same faith and peace of mind is available to Christians today, why don't more of us possess it?

We have covered only those parts of Daniel which are applicable to this study. You may want to read the entire book.

From time to time every Christian is called upon to be an intercessor. The Quakers call it their "bundle"; God puts a real concern in a person's heart for another person, for a situation, for an organization, for her country. When God gives us a "bundle" to carry, we should pray about it until we feel a lifting of that concern. This may mean praying for one day, or it may mean shorter daily prayers over a period of time, days or even years.

As intercessors we have for our inspiration, not only the great heroes of the Bible, but Jesus and the Holy Spirit, both of whom intercede continuously for us. Can we afford to do less?

Personal Application

(1) Do I truly believe that God is no respector of persons, that the miracles of God are as available to me today as they were to Daniel?

(2) What personal qualities did Daniel possess that I might do well to seek for myself?

(3) Daniel was praised for his wisdom and understanding. The spiritual gifts of the Word of Wisdom and Knowledge are available to all Christians today. How can we see a greater operation of them in our lives?
(4) How much am I relying on what others hear from the Lord, rather than hearing His voice directly?

Notebook Assignment

Ask the Lord whom He would have you intercede for. Make a list of the people He lays on your heart and begin praying for them. Be sure you list your requests and the date you began praying for them in the Prayer Request section of your notebook. Watch for results!

Advanced Studies

(1) Psalm 137 speaks of the Babylon captivity. See if you can find evidence of any other Psalms that came out of that period.
(2) The law of the Medes and Persians is mentioned more than once in the Bible. Find out what it was.
(3) Using other resource books find out if there is any record, other than Bible, of Daniel in the history of Babylon.

Enrichment Assignment for Chapter 8.

(1) Both Jesus and Moses fasted for 40 days. Read about these two fasts and compare them.

Memory Work

(1) "Let the name of God be blessed forever and ever, for wisdom and power belong to Him" (Daniel 2:20).
(2) "I in them, and Thou in Me, that they may be perfected in unity, that the world may know that Thou didst send Me, and didst love them, even as Thou didst love Me" (John 17:23).
(3) "Hence, also, He is able to save forever those who draw near to God through Him, since He always lives to make intercession for them" (Hebrews 7:25).
(4) "Likewise the Spirit also helps our infirmities: for we know not what we should pray for as we ought; but the Spirit itself maketh intercession for us with groanings which cannot be uttered" (Romans 8:26).

Lesson Eight
Fasting

Introduction
"Fast and pray." How often these words are linked together in Scripture! But what is this fasting that the Bible talks about? And is it valid for today? If so, who is supposed to fast? When? And for what purpose? Let's find out.

Fasting is the voluntary abstaining from food or certain kinds of food. It has been an important part of the religious observance of the Jews throughout their long history. In Jesus' time, religious Jews fasted at least two days a week.

Prayer: Father, we want to learn all Your ways. Teach us to be open to all new ideas from You.

Discussion Question: Share with the group how you were led in intercession.

Bible Study
The first recorded instance of fasting in the Bible is in the Book of Judges.
Read **Judges 19** and **Judges 20:23-28**.
(1) What was the purpose of this fast? _____

_____.

Read **1 Samuel 7:1-6**.
(2) What was the purpose of this fast? _____.
Read **2 Samuel 12:1-23**.
(3) What was the purpose of David's fast? _____

_____.

The Bible does not record the introduction of the fast in the life of the Israelites. These three references, however, imply that the practice was well-established before the incidents mentioned.
Read **1 Samuel 31:7-13**.
(4) Why did these valiant men fast? _____.

Read **1 Kings 21:20-29**.
(5) Why did King Ahab fast? _____.

(6) What was the result? _____.
Read **Nehemiah 1:1-6**.
(7) Why did Nehemiah fast? _____.
Read **Acts 13:2**.
(8) What happened when the new church was praying? _____
_____.

(9) Based on the information in these Scriptures, what do we find

are the primary purposes for fasting? _____
_____.

Read **Luke 4:1,2,14**.
These verses in Luke are an account of Jesus' forty-day fast.

(10) Why did Jesus fast? _____.
Jesus probably had water to drink during this period because Scripture records that at the end of the forty days He _____.

Discussion Question: Do you think Jesus had supernatural powers that made it easier for him to fast than it is for us?

(11) What does the Scripture say about Jesus when He returned from

the wilderness? _____.
The fasting, rather than being debilitating, was actually empowering when it followed the baptism of the Holy Spirit. The proof of this is in the next statement.

(12) What happened to Jesus after this experience? _____
_____.

Jesus was still in His home country, although not in the same town of His childhood. He was seeing and talking with people who had been with Him before. But now, there was a power in what He said. People began to take notice, even to the extent of telling their friends about Him.

Read **Acts 9:1-9**.
(13) Why do you think Saul (Paul) was fasting? _____
_____
_____.

Notice that vs. 9 says he "neither _____ nor _____.
This is not the usual way to fast but is acceptable for short periods

when the results are urgently needed. Through his training, Paul was a well-disciplined man.

Read 2 Corinthians 11:27.

(14) What distinguishes fasting from the "hunger and thirst" also mentioned? _____.

Read Psalm 35:13.

(15) What reason does the psalmist give for fasting? _____
_____.

It is neither easy nor natural to fast. Our natural inclination is to eat when we are hungry (and sometimes more often than that). When we realize the control that our bodies, our natural desires, have over us, our souls are indeed humbled before God.

Read Acts 13:1-3.

(16) In Acts 13:1-2, who is fasting? _____.

(17) For what purpose? _____.

(18) With what result? _____
_____.

In the New Testament Church, fasting was a normal prelude to seeking God's guidance in the choice of elders and missionaries and in commissioning them to begin their new work.

As we have seen, fasting can also be a valid way of intensifying feelings of repentence, humbling ourselves before God and seeking guidance and blessing on new projects. However, there is a right and a wrong way to fast. See what the Scriptures say about motives and methods.

Read Matthew 6:16-18.

Although our culture is very different than that of Jesus' day, we can still make too big a deal over the externals of our fasting.

(19) What should our appearance be when we fast? _____.

(20) How should we fast? _____.

Discussion Question: When would we not fast secretly?

Read Isaiah 58. (See KJV also).

(21) Why does God say He will not honor their fast? _____
_____.

In the Amplified Bible, "find pleasure" is translated as "find business profit." In other words, fasting combined with "business as usual" is not pleasing to God.

(22) What quality is God objecting to in Verse 4? _____

(23) What is God's purpose for fasting (Verse 5)? _____

(24) What four things does God ask of His people in Verse 6? ___

   The yoke is the harness used for oxen, usually linking two animals together for pulling loads. In ancient times, conquering nations had victory parades, with the victors holding yokes over the heads of the captives to symbolize their new status of slavery. So the yoke can be a symbol of oppression. God says we are to have no oppression in our midst — political, national, financial or physical.

(25) What does God ask in Verse 7? _____

   Notice the last part of Verse 7. While we are not to carry on "business as usual" we are not to lock ourself in a room away from our family, either. This is particularly true if they are not fasting with us. Married women are subject to their husband's guidance as in other things, and it may be necessary to adjust our method of fasting to please our husband.

(26) What are the four rewards mentioned in Verse 8 for an "acceptable fast"? _____

(27) What are the conditions and rewards mentioned in Vs. 9-12? _____

   Feasting is the opposite of fasting and is associated with times of joy. Jesus was criticized because His disciples did not fast as John's

disciples did.
Read **Mark 2:18-20**.
(28) What was Jesus' response to His critics? _____

_____

_____.

Discussion Question: In light of Jesus' response, will there be any fasting in heaven?

Personal Application
(1) Have I sought the Lord to determine whether or not He wants me to fast on a regular basis and/or on specific occasions?
(2) What are some of the aspects of the Lord's "acceptable fast" that I can apply to my own life?
(3) If I am already fasting, have I combined it with "business as usual," seeking my own pleasure, rather than the Lord's?

Notebook Assignment
If you have never fasted before, there is no time like the present to begin! Many experts feel that starting slowly is the best way to proceed. You can begin with the giving up of a single meal or fasting only from solids (liquids permitted). If you want to fast for an entire day, you may find it easier to begin your fast in the evening as the Jews did. Accompany your fast with as much seeking the Lord's will as you can.

Later, you can try longer or more complete fasts. Discuss fasting with the more experienced members of your group. On longer fasts, some preparation before you actually begin may be in order. There is also wisdom in slowly resuming normal eating after a longer fast. Record your reactions, etc. in your notebook.

Advanced Study
(1) Look up information in the United State's history when, on different occasions, the nation has been called to a day of fasting and prayer.
(2) Make a complete study of fasting in the Bible.

Enrichment Assignment for Chapter 9.
(1) Read the entire book of Esther.
(2) Determine exactly when in Israel's history the events of the book took place.
(3) Learn as much as you can about the Babylon Empire and its history, both preceding and following this period.

Memory Work
(1) "Is this not the fast which I chose, to loosen the bonds of

wickedness, to undo the bands of the yoke, and to let the oppressed go free, and break every yoke?" (Isa. 58:6).

(2) "And Jesus returned to Galilee in the power of the Spirit; and news about Him spread through all the surrounding district" (Luke 4:14).

(3) "But you, when you fast, anoint your head, and wash your face so that you may not be seen fasting by men, but by your Father who is in secret; and your Father, who sees in secret will repay you" (Matt. 6:17-18).

Lesson Nine
Esther

Introduction

King Cyrus, who came to power at the end of Daniel's life, had given all captive people permission to return to their homelands. Many Jews returned to the Jerusalem area, but some stayed on where they were. Esther was a member of a family which remained. The king in this book is Ahasuerus, the King Xerxes of history books.

The book of Esther is a strong story of what fasting can do, in collaboration with prayer.

Prayer: Lord, You have said that all Scripture is useful for teaching. Let us be ready to learn what the lives of Your saints of the past have to teach us. Amen.

Discussion Question: Share your fasting experience(s) with your group.

Read **Esther 1.**

(1) Why was Queen Vashti deposed? _____

_____.

(2) What did the letter sent to all the provinces say? _____

_____.

Read **Esther 2.**

(3) What did the king's counselors advise him to do? _____

_____.

(4) How were Esther and Mordecai related? _____

_____.

(5) Describe the circumstances that resulted in Esther's being at the

king's palace. _____

(6) What kind of person was Esther? (See vss. 9, 15, 20) _____

We can see God's hand at work in all the events of this story. Long before He would use Esther to save His people, the Lord set up the circumstances and began preparing Esther for the role she would play.

(7) Did the king know Esther's background? _____.

(8) How did Mordecai continue his care of Esther? _____.

(9) How did Mordecai save the king's life? _____

_____.

Once again God had prepared circumstances far in advance of the time they would be used.

Read **Chapter 3.**

(10) Was Mordecai rewarded for his act? _____.

(11) Who received a promotion shortly afterwards? _____.

(12) Who refused to bow to Haman? _____.

(13) Why did Haman really want to destroy the Jews? _____

_____.

(14) What reason did he give to King Ahasuerus for having the Jews destroyed? _____

_____.

(15) What two things were to be done according to the edict? ____

_____.

(16) What geographical area was covered by the edict? (See Chapter 1, verse 1). _____.

This area probably included all the Jews in the world. Think of it! God's chosen people, the nation which had been promised the

Messiah, was ordered to be wiped out in a single day. Fortunately, the edict did not take effect immediately.

(17) How much time did the Jews have to get it modified or rescinded? _____.

Read **Chapter 4.**

(18) How did the Jews react to the news of the edict? _____

_____.

Notice that word of the edict came to Esther in a round-about way.

Discussion Question: Why do you think Mordecai would choose to do it this way?

(19) What was Esther's reaction to Mordecai's request? _____

_____.

Her reaction was quite human (Remember Queen Vashti!) But Mordecai told Esther she would not be spared. Although the king was still not aware that Esther was a Jewess, Mordecai knew Haman would be very thorough in his research of geneologies.

(20) How did Mordecai reveal his strong trust in God? (v. 14)

_____.

Mordecai touched on an eternal truth here. Esther could choose whether or not she would risk aiding her people. She was not a puppet; she had freedom of choice. But Mordecai reminded her that if she chose not to speak out, she and her father's household would surely be destroyed, but God would send relief and deliverance to the Jews some other way.

Discussion Question: Are God's plans ever dependent upon a single person?

At last Esther realizes the unique position God has placed her in. She recognizes that it is a privilege to be used by God. Although she could not choose the place, the time, nor the circumstances, she would serve Him anyway.

(21) What was her command to Mordecai? _____

_____.

Read **Chapter 5.**

(22) When did Esther attempt to see the king? _____.

(23) What request did she make of the king? _____

_____.

(24) What was Haman's reaction? _____

_____.

(25) What was the one thing that spoiled his happiness? _____

_____.

(26) What did he do when he got home? _____

_____.

(27) What was his wife's suggestion? _____

_____.

Read **Chapter 6.**

See how quickly God moves when He is ready to act! No time is wasted. That very night we see the next step unfold.

(28) What problem did the king have that night? _____.

(29) What did he do? _____.

(30) What did he learn? _____.

The world might call it coincidence, but there are no coincidences with God. Of all the hours day and night that Haman could have arrived at the palace, he "chose" precisely that exact moment.

(31) How did Haman outwit himself? _____

_____.

(32) What was Haman forced to do? _____.

(33) What did Haman's wife and friends say when he told them his

story? _____

_____.

Read **Chapters 7** and **8.**

(34) How was Haman's plot revealed to the king? _____

_____.

(35) What happened to Haman? _____.

One major problem remained, however. Haman's edict had been sealed with the king's ring and according to the law of the Medes and Persians it could not be reversed.

(36) How was this problem overcome? _____

_____.

Read **Chapters 9 and 10.**
(37) Compare the situation of the Jews in Chapters 3 and 9.

Chapter 3 _____

_____.

Chapter 9 _____

_____.

(38) What was the turning point? _____.

Only God knows how many situations have been turned from evil to good when the people of God have prayed and fasted. The anniversary of the day when God spared the lives of His people is called Purim and is still celebrated by Jews today.

Personal Application

(1) Would I be willing to put my life on the line for the Lord if He asked me to?
(2) Do I have Modecai's kind of faith that the Lord will triumph even in the darkest of circumstances?
(3) Do I utilize all the spiritual resources available to me when I go into spiritual battle?

Advanced Studies

(1) Make a study of how Purim is celebrated both in the past and among Jews today.
(2) Learn as much as you can about the marriage customs of Persia and Media during Esther's time.

Notebook Assignment

Become an intercessor for your country. See if the Lord will have you pray for specific situations and people in government or whether you are to pray generally for conditions. Perhaps your study group might agree to pray "with one accord" for certain situations or officials. Keep a running record in your notebook of what you are praying for, the dates and **the results.**

Just because you have finished this study on prayer does not, of course, mean that you will want to stop using your notebook. If you have kept up the assignments so far, you have formed the good habit of keeping records about your prayers and your prayer life. It would be a shame to stop now. Just as you continue to pray, continue to keep your notebook. It will prove to be a blessing both now and in the future.

Memory Work

(1) "And who knows whether you have attained royalty for such a time as this?" (Esther 4:14b).

(2) "Is My hand so short, that it cannot ransom or have I no power to deliver?" (Isa. 50:2b).

(3) "So they will fear the name of the Lord from the west and His glory from the rising of the sun, for He will come like a rushing stream, which the wind of the Lord drives" (Isa. 59:19).

Conclusion

Even in a Bible Study of this nature we can hardly do justice to a subject so broad and as critical to the Christian life as prayer. Some answers to our questions will be found only through experience; others may not be known until we meet the Lord face to face.

Whatever our uncertainties, whatever our doubts, however, one thing we know clearly: when Christians pray, God moves and things begin to happen.

Luke tells us that as the disciples and Jesus prayed on a mountain top, Jesus was transfigured before the disciples' eyes; it was while Cornelius prayed that the Lord spoke to Him and told him to send for Peter; while Paul and Silas prayed and praised the Lord in the Philippian jail, the Lord sent an earthquake that freed them. While he was praying in the Temple in Jerusalem, Paul had a vision and received the call to take the Gospel to the Gentiles.

Today when Christians pray, people are saved, healed and baptized with the Holy Spirit; marriages are mended, children and parents, reunited and broken minds are restored.

Today as we pray, the Lord is putting the final touches to this age. Let us continue to pray!